THE WOMAN I AM

THOUGHTS, POEMS, AND STORIES

*To Hilda
With love
from
Jean*

ISBN: 978-0-692-63842-2

THE WOMAN I AM

THOUGHTS, POEMS, AND STORIES

JEAN JOHNS

Voices heard

Secret places

Years of tears

Set free with words

MY BACKWARD FOREWORD

My friend who is helping me compile my collection of writings asked me to write a foreword.

I didn't want to tell her I didn't know how to write a foreword, so I decided to write a backward and call it My Backward-Foreward.

My expression of life has been a backward-forward experience, really.

I turned 80 in March of this year, 2015, and with the "Grace of God" on my side I might have 10 more years to tap into some lifetime dreams— but I need to hurry it up. There have been many times in the past 80 years when I thought my life was ending.

In 1939, I was four years old when World War II broke out and I remember holding my sister's hand as we watched my parents blotting out light from our windows so the bomber planes couldn't see us. We kept our thoughts to ourselves as we watched the expression of fear in our parents' eyes.

Nuclear war threats played as background noise in the late 50's and into the early 60's. The assassination of President Kennedy in 1963 came as a personal trauma to all of us. We all remembered exactly where we were and the exact moment the shots rang out. Violence continued for the next few years and more assassinations were carried out. Word on the street was, "We'll never make it out of this one alive."

In the mid 80's my friends and I gathered and held hands as we sang on the moonlit beach and prayed for world peace as we celebrated the Harmonic Convergence, as it was known.

On December 31st, 1999 I made sure my garage was stocked with survival food inventory and hundreds of bottles of water ready for the millennium and the possible outcome of the end of life.

I backed up all of my computer files as rumors continued to say the computer would fail because it was not built for the emergence of a new century (something like that). The clock struck 12:00 and we held our breath, awaiting our fate.

Then the turn of the century and one year later, on September 11th, we all watched in disbelief as New York was attacked and the horror of horrors were set before our eyes on the morning news. Everyone had the same thoughts that morning as the terror attacks continued throughout the day. It was surely the end.

Well, here I am some 15 years later writing my Backward-Foreward in these few pages put together from my life as a woman who survived the 50's and a woman blessed with a life of joy beyond belief, an amazing family and a boatload of best friends.

Thank you God.

JEAN JOHNS 2015

THE WOMAN I AM

The woman I am, I am.
        I am the woman I am.
        I am young.
        I am old.
                My hair is gray.
                Neck skin sags.
                Face skin blotches.
                Pubic hair thins.
                Vagina dries.
                Wrinkles and folds all over the place.
        The woman I am, I am.
        I am the woman I am.
The woman I was, I was.
        I was the woman I was.
        Nineteen years a virgin.
        Juicy and ripe.
        Four husbands.
        Five births.
                Full of hormones and juice.
                Juice dripped down my legs.
                Juice all over me, all over my men.
                Juice, juice, juice all over the place.
                The woman I was, I was.
        I was the woman I was.
The woman I am, I am.
        I am the woman I am.
        I am young.
        I am old.
                Eight decades since my birth.
                Healthy mind and spirit.
                Good legs.
                Good face.
                Juices dripping from my soul.
                Writing and drawing all over the place.
        The woman I am, I am.
I am the woman I am.

CHANGE

Change drove me to change.

> "Hang on," she said.
> "This is going to be a fast trip.
>> You cannot stay in this place any longer."

She strapped my seat belt and we took off.
She drove fast.
She drove through stop signs and barricades.
She drove me through passages that were too small.

> "I cannot get through this," I cried.
She drove me through darkness and I saw new faces.

She shifted to overdrive.

> "I want to go back," I screamed.

She set the cruise control.

> "It is too late to go back," she said.
> "We are halfway there.
>> You cannot go back to what was.
>> There is no reverse on this vehicle."

I closed my eyes and prayed to God.

ABDICATION

I gave myself away so many times
I can't remember.
Harmless, innocent, unavailable men
had the power.

I gave my soul to my first husband.
The night he entered me for the first time.
He pushed and it hurt and something broke in my head.
"I am yours," I whispered.

I am yours, I thought as I lay under him.
I don't want to be mine so let me be yours.
I will be whatever you want me to be.
Love me and I will do anything.

Giving Up Me To Be Loved By You.

My song.

My song of abdication.
My song of life.

THE BATHROOM FLOOR

It was May 1, 1974.

I was lying crosswise on my bed still fully clothed in my parka, boots and jeans. My attention was drawn to the curtains moved by the breeze in the open window over my bed. I stared at the tall pine trees that nested our new home in the Sierra Nevada Mountains, so graceful and dignified as they yielded to the wind. I moved my head slightly and realized that my face was stuck to the bedspread. I saw that I had been sick on myself and immediately the thoughts began, "Oh my God, not again." I peeled my face from the bedspread and slid onto the floor and crawled to the bathroom. I stood up and as I looked in the mirror I stared at an image I did not recognize. Both eyes were bruised black and blue, my hair was matted in the sickness and the eyelash I so carefully glued to my left eyelid the night before was now hanging from my left cheek. Momentarily shocked into reality, thoughts of my life began to run like a black and white movie. I wondered what happened to that young woman in her cheerleading outfit, her virgin marriage, her Doris Day life in her organdy apron, her white eyelet lampshades, her wagon wheel on her front lawn and her children's freshly polished white shoes. The blood drained from my head and I fell to my knees on the bathroom floor. "God, help me," I cried.

Was this God I was praying to the same God I thought I would find when I was 13 years old, walking to the pulpit to save my soul, wrapped in a sheet by Reverend Pryor and dunked into the baptism pool? Was it the same God I was looking for when I was 16 and went to church with my best friend, Dori, and held her rosary beads? Was it the same God I had prayed to just the week before when lying on the staircase of our home and crying in quiet desperation?

Living in a ski resort town was a different lifestyle than any I had ever known. Drinking alcohol anytime of the day or night was acceptable and made me look less obvious. We owned our own bar restaurant and drinking with the customers became a nightly event along with Bloody Marys at Fuzz's Place for lunch and, of course, a beer at ski breaks up on the mountain was not unusual. I thought I had found my place in the world.

I don't know if prayers are heard and if they are answered by God, but that morning in May changed my life. A phone call from my dear friend, Jerry Lu, and a trip to my hometown of Santa Barbara to a meeting of Alcoholics Anonymous answered my lifetime quest to know a God of my own understanding. I found that God on the bathroom floor.

IF I WERE A TREE

If I were a tree
I could live by the creek
I wouldn't brush my teeth, not for a whole week
I could watch the frogs jump over the logs
And my big brother Ben
Couldn't whack me again.
      If I were a tree
      I could live in the sky
      I could dance with the clouds as they go by
      I could play with the wind, I could wiggle my branches
      I could scare little boys
      If they played with matches.
If I were a tree
I could live underground
I could watch the ants
Running round and round
I could watch the squirrels, the gophers too
It would be like living inside a zoo.
      If I were a tree
      I'd be tall and strong
      And no one could tell me
      I was ever wrong
      Mom wouldn't tell me pick up my toys
      And dad wouldn't tell me not to make so much noise.
If I were a tree
I could live in the woods
I could play in the sun
I could have so much fun
I could hold all the birds, they could build their nests
We could talk without words, they could come there to rest.
      If I were a tree
      Then mom and dad wouldn't have me
      And that would be sad
      So I guess I will stay
      Who I am today
      But maybe tomorrow, I'll be a tree, okay?

SHADES OF GRAY

I am moving from black and white
To take up residence in shades of gray.
Will everything be the same?
Will dawn still turn to dusk and dusk to dawn?
Or will everything be meaningless and mundane?

Black and white is where I've lived.
I know the smells, the corridors, the hiding places.
I know the way in and the way out.
It's up or it's down, it's here and then it's gone.
And it's always the same at this address.

Shades of gray is my residence now.
There are no more hiding places, no more dark corridors.
Dawn is still turning to dusk and dusk is still turning to dawn.
It goes up, it comes down and then it moves to the middle.
And it's the same and never the same at this address.

FOR RON
February 12, 1957 – June 17, 2005

My son died on a Friday.
I held onto his legs as he slipped from my grasp.
He opened his eyes as he took his last breath
And passed from life into the unknown.

I placed his large capable hands in mine
And cried my tears into them.
He was my first born son
And now a burly, bearded, six-foot-two man with a ponytail.

They closed the curtains,
Behind this screen, his lifeless body.
My heart broken as I walked away.
Never to touch his skin again.

I drove to the beach.
I dug my toes into the sand and looked up
into the nothingness that had swept my son away.
"Where are you Ron?" I shouted to the ocean.

I pulled two Snickers bars from my pocket.
The chocolate soothed the pain in my throat.
"Shall I eat yours too?"
The ocean wave touched my toes.
"OK," I cried as I swallowed the last bite.

And I knew he was there.

MOTHER

Oh dear Mother
  I look at your face
I see my own staring back
   You have grown so small
   Your bed is too big for you
   Your hands are closed and tight
   Your feet are cold
   Your eyes open and close without focus.
Are you scared, Mother?
Or is it me there I see there in your face?

I remember your breasts when they were filled with milk.
The milk was sweet and it overflowed in my mouth.
   Your voice was soft and lovely.
You loved me then.

I want to steal you away from this place.
Away from the halls filled with sadness.
   And sing you to sleep with lullabies.
Where you will be wrapped in God's grace

        forevermore.

EST

After my divorce I went to EST. I wore my red jump suit, my gold earrings and told all my secrets. Ellie, my best friend, took EST after her divorce told all her secrets and it transformed her life. She got thin, wore tight jeans and streaked her hair. She also talked different. She told me that I was an unconscious asshole and that was why my life was not working. She said I needed to sign up for the EST training to become enlightened. She said in EST, an asshole is a term used to describe people that didn't "get it."

Ellie took me to the introductory seminar at the Biltmore Hotel in Santa Barbara. I paid $300 to the EST trainer. I signed up for the summer of '75 session which was to be held the following two weekends in the Embassy Room at the Hilton Hotel in Los Angeles.

The first weekend seminar began at 8:00am the following Saturday. I was 20 minutes late and one the trainers stopped me at the door and said,

"You have broken an agreement by being late and when you break an agreement in EST you will be expected to look at what gets in the space between you and fulfilling your agreements. Your life works to the degree to which you keep your agreements, and it is obvious that your life is not working."

He sounded just like Ellie. When the training session began, I was so scared I would be one of the ones that didn't "get it". I told all my secrets and some secrets I didn't even have.

Ellie came to my graduation on the Sunday night of the second weekend. I asked her why I didn't feel transformed and why I still felt like an asshole.

She said, "If we don't acknowledge we are assholes because somewhere in our belief system we are hanging on to *it's bad to be an asshole* then we are really assholes—and—it doesn't make any difference. An asshole is someone who is resisting being an asshole."

I didn't see Ellie for the next ten years. She moved to Los Angeles and became an EST trainer. Some of my fellow EST graduates that didn't "get it" saw her from time to time and referred to her as a real ESTHOLE.

I didn't hear from her for ten years. She called last week and told me she was living in Newhall, California. She sounded like the good old Ellie I used to know. She said she was remarried, her fat was back and she was very happy. We joked about our EST days. I have often wondered why she "got it" and I didn't. Maybe it was because her secrets were better than mine.

MADAME ROSINKA

"You are going to feel a lot different the day you see him with his new girlfriend," my attorney said with a frown as he pushed the papers across the desk for me to sign.

"I don't want anything from him," I shouted as I pushed the papers back with my signature.

I only wish I hadn't driven by Bob's house that day. I wish I hadn't seen him drive off in his new GTS with the sunroof and his new girlfriend sitting next to him.

My attorney was right, I did feel different that day.

Bob and I had just celebrated his 50th birthday and our 10th wedding anniversary with a trip to Hawaii. It was May of 1982. We drove to Los Angeles from our home in Santa Barbara for an early flight.

"Why are you always late?" he said as he threw our luggage in the trunk of our car.

He seemed agitated and when I tried to talk to him, he mostly scowled and ignored whatever I said to him. We arrived at the Royal Hawaiian Hotel, in Waikiki in late afternoon and memories of our past days in this place came flooding to my mind. We entered our room and I immediately threw off my clothes and approached him to make love.

"I am not in the mood for that," he said as he turned away, put his swim trunks on and headed for the beach.

I put my bathing suit on and followed him. I laid my towel down on the beach next to him and he got up immediately and went in the water. We had dinner in the hotel dining room that night. It was our anniversary dinner.

"Can you believe we have been together 10 years?" I said to him dreamily.

"No," he answered as he took a sip of his wine.

We went to bed that night and Bob was asleep by the time I finished in the bathroom. I woke up at 7:00 and I rolled over and curled my body around his and began to rub his back.

"Come for a swim with me," I said in my most soft and sexy voice.

"It's too early," he grumbled and pulled the covers over his head as to not engage with me. There was no more mention of the anniversary after that.

The next night I arranged a birthday celebration at the restaurant next to our hotel for his birthday. I wore my new black sun dress with spaghetti straps and the white Puka shell beads Bob had given me on our first trip to Hawaii 5 years ago on our 5th year anniversary.

"I don't want to celebrate this birthday," his voice raised to a higher pitch than normal as we walked to the restaurant.

I didn't want to tell him I had already arranged a birthday celebration with the restaurant and planned a pineapple cheesecake which I paid for in advance. When the waiter placed the cake in front of Bob after dinner complete with candles and a "Happy 50th Birthday" written in bright purple, he looked at me with a sneer and blew out the candles as to not draw attention. He then pushed the plate aside, and whispered with clenched teeth,

"I told you I didn't want to celebrate this birthday, don't you get it?"

The rest of the meal was in silence.

The next night we had a fish dinner at the Hula Grill, one of our favorite places to eat. When we returned to our hotel we walked by the bar and we heard the band playing, "Hurt So Good." John Mellencamp was one of our favorite musicians and we had danced to his music many times over the years.

"Do you want to dance?" I asked as I turned to Bob motioning a dance move. There was no response and we walked slowly to our room with no more words between us.

We boarded the plane for our flight home and as we walked down the aisle to our seats he spotted a vacant seat in the back of the plane.

"Is anyone sitting there?" he asked the flight attendant.

"Wait until everyone boards and I will let you know."

He moved to the vacant seat and as I buckled my seat belt I felt the anxiety and pain welling up in my throat. I watched a movie and when that was over I turned to the man sitting next to me.

"Do you live in the Los Angeles area?" Trying to keep my mind occupied and off the reality of what was really happening.

"Santa Barbara, really? That's where I live too, well, I mean that's where my husband and I live."

I could see the man had no interest in further conversation so I turned to my magazine for the rest of the flight. We arrived in Los Angeles at 10:00 pm and as we were exiting the baggage claim area, Bob yelled,

"I can't remember which parking lot we are in." He fumbled with the papers in his briefcase becoming more and more agitated.

"Why can't you pay more attention to things?" "You always leave it up to me to find the car in this God damn place."

There was complete silence on our drive home to Santa Barbara. When we arrived home, Bob went straight to our bedroom and began throwing clothes into another suitcase.

"What are you doing?" I screamed, now fully aware of the reality of the situation.

"I am tired of you, I am tired of this marriage, I am tired of your dependency on me for everything, you don't assert yourself, I am tired of 10 years and the same old thing and I want my freedom and I don't love you anymore."

I fell to my knees and cried,

"Please don't leave." Then I begged.

"I will be better, I promise will try to be better."

To my disbelief, he walked out the front door with two suitcases, one in each hand with pieces of clothing sticking out the sides. I stood in the doorway with a towel over my face to hold back the would-be screams as he drove off. I stood frozen for a few moments as I watched the car turn the corner and then ran back into the house and called Katie, my best friend and mentor who had just moved to Tucson, Arizona.

"Katie," I sobbed, "I know it's late but Bob just packed his stuff and walked out and told me he doesn't love me anymore and he wants a divorce and I am not assertive enough and I depend on him too much and he wants his freedom and he doesn't love me anymore and…"

Katie interrupted me,

"Oh sweetie, I am so sorry," the sound of her voice was comforting in that moment.

"I can't believe it, you seemed happy—what happened—oh sweetie, I am so sorry," she repeated with her warm southern drawl.

"I don't know, Katie, I can't stop crying and I don't know what to do"

"Well sweetheart, I will tell you what to do right now, you just hang up the phone and call and get reservations and fly down here tomorrow morning and be with me this weekend."

"Ok," I said as I hung up the phone.

I called and made reservations to fly to Tucson the next morning at 5:30am. I crawled in bed with my clothes on holding the phone close to my chest in case it rang with different news from Bob. I set the alarm for 4:00 before dozing into a half sleep.

Katie picked me up at the Tucson airport and before I could settle into my seat and fasten my seat belt she said, "You know sweetie, this could be just a coincidence but I was reading the newspaper this morning and saw something interesting. There is an Assertiveness Training Seminar at the Tucson Hilton and it starts tomorrow morning and goes to Sunday evening. It sounds like it might be just the thing you need right now so I called and registered you."

"Oh Katie," I cried. "There is no way I can do anything like that in this condition."

"Well sweetie, I know how you feel but I think you need some help with certain things in your life and I have a good feeling about this."

Katie was not only my friend and mentor, she was my AA sponsor and I learned to trust her guidance over the years, however, this idea seemed impossible to me.

We arrived at her home from the airport and she immediately made me a cup of tea and we settled into a day of tears and lots of reassuring dialogue. After dinner she led me to the bathroom and drew a hot bath as she poured drops of lavender from her collection of aroma therapy bottles on the shelf.

"You get a good night's rest sweetie and I think you will feel different in the morning,"

She walked me to her guest room, tucked me into her large four poster bed between her 1000 count sheets and a fluffy down comforter. I sunk into the down pillows and cried,

"OK, Katie, I will do it. I will go tomorrow, I will do it."

She dropped me at the front door of the Hilton in downtown Tucson the next morning. The room was filled and I found a seat in the back of the room and sat down quickly. I removed my sun glasses and the women sitting next to me said, "Oh here dear, I brought extra tissues."

"Thank you," I said as I looked down so others could not see my red eyes.

"*Assertive people*," the speaker began, "*are doers, they get things done.*"

He was handsome and young and his well-groomed preppy style made it easier to hear his message from the stage. He continued in his smooth, soft voice as he stepped from the stage into the audience.

"*Empowered people do whatever it takes to find the best solution. They are less stressed and they know they have personal power and they don't feel threatened or victimized when things don't go as planned.*"

He walked directly toward the woman sitting next to me. I ducked my head further into my Kleenex and put my sun glasses back on. He held the microphone in front of the two of us and then looked directly at me,

"It looks to me like we have a young lady here needing help with some of these issues we have been discussing today. Is there anything you would like to share about yourself with the audience today?"

I got up from my seat, pushed by him and ran to the lobby. I dialed Katie's number from the pay phone.

"Come get me right now," I yelled. I ran out of Kleenex so I ran to the ladies room and pulled paper towels from the dispenser and went to wait for her in front of the building.

"What happened, sweetie?" she said as she pulled away from the curb in front of the hotel. "I thought this might help you to feel better."

"Well, it didn't," I sobbed. "I don't want to learn how to be assertive, Katie, I just want to die and get it over with."

"Oh dear. Well, let's go home and I'll fix you some dinner and you can just rest for the rest of the weekend." Katie cooked me a pot of Black Eyed Peas for dinner and I began to feel comforted just being with her in her home.

I flew home Monday morning to an empty house and felt I would burst wide open with the grief and fear. I bent over the kitchen counter holding my face in my hands, the tears falling onto the newspaper on the counter. Through my blurred vision I saw:

MADAME ROSINKA – PALM READER
PSYCHIC – SPIRITUAL – CONSULTANT

I called the number and a woman with broken English answered.

"Yez darlink," she said after listening to me for a minute or two.

"You have forty dolar read from me or eighty dolar read, eighty dolar is Za Vorks."

I chose the $40.00 session just to be safe and made an appointment for that afternoon.

"Dis guy, who is dis guy makes you cry?" She asked as she studied my palms.

"Vy you vant dis guy? Vat good is he? He is boy dressed as man."

I decided I needed the $80.00 session and told her I wanted "The Works." This time she studied my palms with more intensity.

"A new guy—I see new guy. He is better for you and he is rich and beautiful—much better for you. Oh and by de vay, Da old guy vill vant to come back to you and you vill have to decide which guy you vant."

I was glad I decided to spend the extra $40.00.

My family came for Thanksgiving dinner that year. It was the first Thanksgiving in 10 years without Bob. I started to cry in the middle of dinner and ran to my room. My mother followed me and sat on the edge of my bed.

"I don't know what to do with my life," I cried as I buried my head in the pillow.

"Well," my mother said, "You can always go to computer school dear," as she patted my back.

"I can't go to computer school, mother, I can't even work my Cuisinart."

It's been a few years since Bob left and Madame Rosinka was right, he did want to come home again.

Eventually "Za new guy" came along just as Madame Rosinka foretold, and that's when I knew it was the best $80.00 I've ever spent.

MY NIGHT LOVER

You are nameless in your black fog.
Silent as you wait for me each night.
Jealous of my other lover.
You take me to your black cave and embrace me with pain.

You keep me in darkness.
You grip my throat and bind my mouth.
You tell me not to speak and not to write.
You threaten me with the death of my children.

My lover of sixty years, how will I leave you?
Will I be lonely and long for your return?
What will happen when I close my eyes?
Will the darkness lead me to your cave again?

I left my Night Lover last night.
I went to the center of life.
I heard the silence and I was safe.
Wrapped in light and embraced by God.

4:26 AM

My bedside clock ticks away at life,
Each tick a reminder of its arrogance.

Helpless to pause and rewind
Once again my bed becomes the battleground

of thoughts.

ODE TO A FIREMAN

He was a hell of a man.

Straightforward, honest, manly and high-principled.
Looked just like the guy in the Lucky Strike ad.
Had the respect of every man on the job.
He was captain of the A Shift at Engine 27 in Hollywood.
Other firemen called him Benchy because his legs were short.

He was a hell of a golfer.
He could "get down in one" with his chipping and putting.
Wasn't bad at baseball either.
He was captain of the "Big Red Team" from Hollywood.
Played handball so hard, the toenails on his big toes fell off every six months.

He fell through a burning building onto a live wire when he was forty.
The other firemen cut him loose.
His picture was in the paper.
He was wrapped up like a mummy and looked like he was dead.
The paper said he survived because he was such a strong man.

Benchy's tan is gone now.
The skin on his arms hangs down.
His chest droops and his shoulders hunch over.
Rivers of veins bulge out of his once strong hands.
He talks about old times and his eyes water and his lips quiver.

When I visited him in the hospital.
I walked by the nursery and glanced at the newborns.
I thought about that March afternoon when I met Benchy for the first time.

My mother told me the story.
She said he held me in a pink blanket and sang,

I dream of Jeanie with the light brown hair.

"Ralph Johns, who spent 40 years battling blazes in the Southland,
died Friday," the obituary said.

He was a hell of a man.

STUNNED

Stunned, I sat up in bed and stared at the man standing over me,
    who looked to be my twin.

"Who are you?" I asked, "And what are you doing here?"

He smiled and answered, "I have come to rescue you from yourself."

LEFTOVERS

I never thought of myself as a "leftover," but my Dad used to say, "Leftovers are better, richer and tastier, there's nothin like 'em." When I began to think of how my dad felt about leftovers I thought, "Well, that's what I am, a leftover." I am aged with good spices and rich memories that have forever left their mark and obviously what didn't spoil or kill me made me better and maybe even tastier. You might say I was ripened on the vine, stewed, canned, pickled and marinated and now 80 years old, maybe much more palatable.

When I think of "ripening on the vine," I think of those pre-teen years when I was ten and eleven years old and we lived next to the Altree Family. They had three children, two older sons and a daughter, Bonnie, the youngest of the three. She was fifteen, and she looked like a movie star. She was tan and her blonde hair was tied back in pony tails with ribbons to match her outfits. She smelled like Johnson's Baby Oil and Prell Shampoo and she shaved her legs and she had breasts. I watched her breasts all the time. We played Croquet on our front lawn every day and when she bent over to hit the croquet ball her breasts fell over her halter top and I held my breath every time hoping to catch a glimpse of one of her nipples. On Saturdays we went to the Chrystal Plunge on Kester Street and she rode me on the handlebars of her bike and I could feel her nipples under her bathing suit as they rubbed my back when she peddled.

That summer and the next were mostly spent worrying about the inverted breasts under my tee shirt. Now as I look back, I would reassure that little ten year old girl she would indeed someday ripen with breasts of her own.

ME

Look in the mirror and you will see

The remnants of what used to be me

I pleased, I pleased, I pleased some more

Until all that was left was a thing

on the floor

That thing on the floor is my flesh and blood

But what's inside is pleased out mud

MY MOTHER'S LEGACY

The soldiers of darkness came when I was ten.
They came and they locked me up tight.
They guarded my shame.
They never slept.

"Did it feel good?" Mother asked.
"No," I replied.
The soldiers came that night.
They wouldn't let me sleep.

"You are guilty," they said.
"You are shameful."
"You lied to your Mother."
"You will never sleep again."

The fist time I slept with Uncle,
I wore my Carmen Miranda pajamas.
I was ten years, old he was fifty.
He touched me where it felt good.
I slept.

It was seventy years ago when the soldiers first came.
They still stand guard.
They are growing old now.
Sometimes they sleep.

And I eat popcorn.

"Clouds Above", oil on canvas by Lisa Paulick Miller

WHERE ARE YOU?

Oh God, where are you?
I am wrapped in myself tonight.
Praying with empty words.

Be still and know that I am God, you whispered.

How do I know for sure?
How do I know you are there?
How do I know?

I am in the silence of your breath.
I am in the ocean waves below and the clouds above.
You are never alone.

SENSATION

Chrishnamurti said, "Sensation is a thing of the mind, not the heart."

I had been meditating on these words for days.

"Sensation is a thing of the mind, not the heart."

I prayed for a deeper understanding.

I returned to the place of my dreams this morning (my bed).

As I pulled the covers back there was the TV remote,

An empty bowl of ice cream and my vibrator.

I suddenly understood Chrishnamurti's message.

God had once again answered with humor.

FROGS

The stillness screams for my attention.
And the frogs haven't sung since May, or was it June?

Who is that man on the beach?
Is it my father, is it my son?

"Come rescue me," I called to the man on the beach.
"I am too busy," answered my son.

"Come rescue me," I called to the man on the beach.
"Why don't you write like Agatha Christie," answered my father.

The stillness speaks again.

Mother Earth is breathing short rasping breaths.
Her breathing has changed.
She's giving way to the pressure.

I am consumed by the stillness.
Swallowed whole.

I am inside. I am alone.

I have returned to the beginning.

WE WERE AFRAID TO GO TO SHIRLEY'S HOUSE AFTER SHE DIED

Her mother told us Shirley was an angel now and she had wings and she flew down every night to drink the lemonade her mother left for her on the windowsill.

Shirley was my older sister Joan's best friend. They belonged to Brownie Troop 8. They had their Brownie meetings every Wednesday after school in the bungalow behind the auditorium. They were supposed to have their bridging fly-up ceremony to become Girl Scouts the week Shirley died. Their Brownie leader told them the ceremony would be postponed because of Shirley's passing.

Shirley's mother wanted Brownie Troop 8 to walk beside the casket at the funeral. Joan cried and said she didn't want to go, but Mother said we had to go to pay our last respects. Shirley's sister told us Shirley died from Romantic Fever.

Reverend Pryor gave the sermon at the funeral.

"She was a good Brownie," he said. "She is in heaven now but will fly down for the fly-up ceremony next week."

Shirley's casket was open and she was lying on a white satin pillow. Her eyes were closed. Her Brownie beanie was on the side of her head and her hair was in ringlets around her shoulders. She was wearing a Brownie dress, and her Brownie badge was pinned to her collar. She had on her Brownie socks and her brand new Mary Jane shoes. She was holding yellow daisies in her hands.

When we got home from the funeral Joan started to cry and said,

"I don't want to be a Brownie anymore, I don't want to be a Girl Scout and I am not going to the fly-up ceremony either." She stuffed all of her Brownie things in a paper bag.

"I am giving this to Charlotte," she sobbed.

Charlotte was also a member of Brownie Troop 8 but she didn't have a uniform because her mother didn't have enough money to buy her one.

I was glad Joan wasn't going to be a Brownie anymore. I was glad she wasn't going to the fly-up ceremony. I was afraid if she did she might become an angel and get wings like Shirley and fly-up forever.

SADNESS

Sadness comes to visit this morning.
It came last night but I locked it out.
I locked it out and ate ice cream.
It came again this morning and I was too tired.
I said, Come in.

I am too tired.

Come into me, I said to sadness.
Come inside me, into my veins, into my heart.
No more fighting and running away.
No more locked doors and starvation.
No more darkness.

I am too tired.

Sadness said, Stay here with me and don't run away.
Stay here and I will come inside you.
I will plant new seeds.
I will fertilize your soul and we will grow new poems.
Stay with me and we will find home.

EAT YOUR GREENS

"They're here, they're here," we screamed when we saw our grandparent's black car turn onto our street at the corner.

We jumped up and down, our bare feet burning as we ran up the street to meet them. They were driving their new car, a 1941 Packard Clipper with running boards and large windows and we could see the back seat filled with luggage and boxes we knew were full of gifts for us.

It was the summer of 1945. I was ten years old and my sister was twelve.

"Took us a damn week to get here," grandpa grumbled through his half eaten cigar as he stepped from the driver's seat and stretched his legs.

We hugged and kissed them and couldn't wait to get them inside. They arrived right on schedule on the evening of August 10th to be with us for two months to take care of the family as our mother was in her last month of pregnancy, and expecting the baby late in September.

We unloaded their things and helped them to settle into our small den with the fold out couch. Our mother prepared a pot roast, our grandpa's favorite meal. She simmered it all day in her cast iron pot and when she placed it on the dining room table and removed the lid the smell caught us all in a moment—almost like prayer time.

"Ummmm," grandpa sighed as he sat down and looked at the meal about to be served to us. The meat and veggies were now a shiny caramel color from bathing in the gravy all day.

Grandpa sat at the head of the table and winked at mother, his mouth filled with pot roast.

"Don't know why people make a big deal over being married 50 years."

Their long drive to California was to care take our family but to also celebrate their 50th wedding anniversary with their family and friends. They drove 1500 miles from their farm in Meadow, Nebraska.

Our grandpa was Jasper Lee Pope. His family and friends called him Bud. Grandma was Lessie Dalmatia Pugh before she married Bud, then she became Lessie Dalmatia Pope. Our mother showed us pictures and enclosures from her family album the day before our grandparents arrived.

"This is what they looked like on their wedding day," she said as she pulled their wedding picture from the album. It was the first time we had seen our grandparents name in print.

Grandma was up early and in the kitchen the next morning.

"Lessie Dalmatia Pugh—Lessie Dalmatia Pugh"—We sang teasingly knowing from our mother's stories, how much our grandmother hated her name. We peered around the corner of the kitchen so she couldn't reach us.

"Get out of here, you little rascals," she yelled as she grabbed a dishtowel and shooed us from the kitchen.

We ran giggling at her threats. She was busy that morning cooking our oatmeal and baking fresh biscuits. Grandma's oatmeal was creamy and soft and when she plopped it into our bowls she added a pat of butter and some honey and rich cream from the top of the milk bottle.

"Move over," my sister said as she pushed me to grab the first bowl. Grandma's love was dished out to us in a bowl of warm, smooth, texture and taste.

Every day we planned extra tricks to play on our grandma. One morning I climbed into our mother's tea table with wheels and my sister pushed me into the kitchen and quickly ran out before grandma could turn around. When grandma did turn around she was startled to see the tea table appear out of nowhere and when she found me hiding on the underneath shelf and heard us giggling she shouted,

"You little devil girls, go on now," once again using the dishtowel as a threat, the most accessible weapon at her disposal.

Grandpa had a black onyx pocket knife that hung from a chain hooked to his belt hook. He spent most of his time that summer sitting on the back porch, whittling. He wore black pants that had shiny patches where he sat. When he got up he had shavings hanging from the seat of his pants and when my sister and I laughed at him he stuck out his false teeth and chased us.

"Come back here, you little varmints."

Breathing heavily he muttered, "I'll catch you two—just wait." He sat down in the lawn chair in the front yard and took a deep breath. We hid in the bushes and stayed there until he went back in the house.

Grandpa and I were sitting on the back porch one day when we heard my mother yell from the laundry room,

"Get this cheese out of here."

Grandpa jumped up ran to the laundry room and grabbed the package of limburger he had hidden on the shelf above the water heater. He brought it back to the porch, sat down and held the cheese up to his nose, sniffed it smiled and said,

"Ahhhhh."

He lowered it down to me and I covered my face. He pulled his knife out and cut the cheese into bite size pieces. He stuck the end of the shiny blade into one of the pieces and put it in his mouth. He closed his eyes and chewed slowly until all the pieces were gone. Then he popped his teeth out and cleaned the remaining pieces from each tooth with the tip of the blade.

"It's nap time," he said as he yawned and got up from the porch.

He took his handkerchief from his back pocket as I had seen him do so many times before and carefully wiped the blade and handle of his knife. He closed it with a familiar "click" and put it in his pocket. Soon I heard him snoring from the bedroom window.

"You eat your greens, Bud Pope."

It was Sunday dinner time and grandma was standing over grandpa with her arm outstretched pointing to the bowl of greens on the dining room table, her voice commanding as it was when she spoke to grandpa. She was in a freshly starched housedress, zipper up the middle; her white cotton apron outlined with black piping covered most of the dress. Each day was a different housedress and each day a fresh apron. She picked greens from our back yard garden—spinach, beet tops, mustard greens and whatever else was green—boiled them, poured them into a large bowl and covered them with butter and vinegar.

Grandpa was sick that year. He had a deep hole in the back of his neck. The doctor said it was caused from diabetes. Every night after dinner Grandma washed the sore and applied new dressings and reminded him about the evils of sugar.

"Hold still," she said, as she wrapped his neck with a fresh bandage.

Grandpa looked longingly at the fresh baked rhubarb pie mother had just brought from the oven and he sang and tapped his foot to one of his favorite songs, "Yankee Doodle Boy."

"It's a boy," our grandma announced as she lowered the phone to her chest.

"Finally your dad gets a son after three girls."

"We have a brother, we have a brother," we screamed as we jumped up and down on the couch much like we did the year before when we heard the news our baby sister was born.

Grandpa grabbed my hands and waltzed me across the room as he sang one of his favorite songs:

Beautiful, beautiful brown eyes.
Beautiful, beautiful brown eyes.
Beautiful beautiful brown eyes
I'll never love blue eyes again.

The wedding anniversary party was October 15th and our home was filled with friends and family.

"Smile and say cheese," the photographer said.

Grandma and grandpa stood in back of a three-tiered cake that sat on our dining table on the day of the celebration. Grandma was dressed in her black rayon dress. You could barely see her pearl necklace under the fringed collar of her dress. Her feathered hat sat to the back of her head and the veil hung over her forehead and her corsage was a white orchid. Grandpa was dressed in his black suit, blue medallion tie, and black Fedora, with a white carnation on his lapel.

"Can we please go home with them," we begged. My sister was holding grandma's hands in hers as they pulled out of the driveway that October day.

"We will go visit them soon," mother said softly as she wiped my tears and took my sister's hand.

They left to go back to their farm four weeks after my brother was born, September 24th.

They visited us one more time before grandpa died in 1954. Grandma went to live with her son in Utah and passed away five years later.

THE BLESSINGS OF 2005

Death of my son: June 13th.
Heart Attack: September 28th, diagnosed as "Broken Heart Syndrome."

My heart has been broken and opened at the same time. I see and feel life in a different way.

First came anger and resentment (still there to a degree) no longer wanting to be in this world. No longer wanting to be with family or friends. Sleepless nights. Terrifying fear and anxiety. Wanting to be where I could isolate and be with the ocean exclusively.

Acceptance of the mundane.
Acceptance of life on life's terms.
Acceptance of powerlessness.
Surrendering to God.

How can I do that?

I hate the mundane every day existence. I hate accepting that I am powerless.

I hate surrendering to God. Basically, I feel as though God has forsaken me.

In all of this pain I see a light. I don't know if it's God or not, but it is a light. The light gives me a metaphor to ponder. I read about it in a book titled *Being Comfortable With Uncertainty*. When my friend recommended this book to me, my reaction was, "Being comfortable with—what?" The metaphor is the idea that we spend our life climbing the mountain to spiritual enlightenment trying to transcend pain and suffering, trying to leave our worldly attachments behind. We find at the top of the mountain our suffering continues, unrelieved by our attempted personal escape. Then the metaphor speaks of what true spiritual enlightenment is. It is the journey down the mountain. As though the mountain points toward the earth instead of the sky. Instead of transcending the suffering of all creatures, we move toward turbulence and doubt however we can. We try to no longer push unpredictability or insecurity and pain away from us. At the bottom of this mountain we find healing water.

In the process of coming down the mountain (feels more like falling down the mountain) my heart is beginning to heal. "Right down there in the thick of things," as the author so eloquently puts it, I am finding love does not die.

This is to my loving family and friends who have been there for me this past year. I think it has probably been much like trying to love a "prickly pear."

DECEMBER 31, 2006

MY SOUL LIES IN WAITING

My soul lies in waiting

Wrapped in a blanket of love

Gently filled with God's grace

My Soul cries out

Embrace me with the divine

Nurture me with your love

Hold me in your embrace

Breathe me with your breath

And I am filled with God's eternal light.

UNDERSTANDING LIFE

draw a picture of life
with chalk

no lines, no boundaries
some colors, some circles
off the page in all directions
life is in there somewhere
just not visible to others

all leading somewhere and nowhere

to God.

UNCLE BRICK

Uncle Brick and malted milk
It tasted good
It felt good
No it didn't

Malt shop before nap
Before Aunt Aura got home
It felt good
No it didn't

I wanted to go home
To Mother and Daddy
No you didn't
Yes I did

I didn't want to tell on Uncle Brick
Yes you did, no you didn't
It felt good
No it didn't.

BALANCE

Balancing on the "Ball of Life".

My toes are tired from holding on.

I let go and keep moving at the same time.

I move and let go, move and let go.

And pray.

MOTHER EARTH

God's illegitimate daughter
Born out of wedlock
Abandoned, seduced and raped
Mother of all, breathing us her breath
Feeding us from her great bosom

She has grown weary
She shouts out the warnings
Her heaven's breezes, no longer sweet
Her cracks and crevices grow deeper
Her sweet milk poisoned

She cries out, AWAKEN!
Come cleanse me and feed me
Love and caress me
Fill my cracks and crevices
I am your savior, I will bring you peace

She sleeps the night.

RON'S ASHES

His ashes were sealed in a finely crafted wooden box made by his father. I stepped into the canoe on the shore of Twin Lakes holding the box close to my chest. It was September 29, 2011. 4:00pm in the afternoon. The sun was dull behind a white cloud almost opalescent in contrast to the sky. The sunbeams danced off the waterfall in the distance and filtered through the pines surrounding the lake. It seemed as though this outdoor canopy of beauty was staged properly for this very moment.

I was the only one on the lake that day except for the ducks that swam around our canoe speaking to me with their noise and splashes and quacks as though they were making up for the silence.

I unsealed the box with a borrowed pocket knife, my heart pounding as I reached inside and felt his ashes for the first time. He was encased in a plastic bag inside the wooden box. I cupped my hand and filled it with part of his remains. Without warning his ashes and bones came alive in my hand and flashbacks of his birth came rushing through my body and I felt that burst of water and his cord between my thighs that had come gushing out moments before his birth cutting off his air.

My tears dropped onto the ashes in my hand. I sprinkled the first handful into the water and watched them slowly drift away following in the duck's wake. My legs began to tremble and the box and the bag of ashes fell from my lap into the bottom of the canoe.

"Oh my God," I screamed.

As I leaned down to pick up the box and the bag I saw that a handful of ashes had spilled onto my right foot. I stared at his ashes resting there on my foot and they seemed to have melded into me and for moments we seem to be one of the same body. I secured myself into the canoe, this time holding my son tightly. My legs were still shaking as I remembered the pain of his birth that still seemed to be lodged there in my thighs. I remembered the screams and the nurses and the doctors rushing and whispering as they positioned the gas on my face covering my nose and mouth. I fought and screamed for my breath until the pain demanded that I surrender to the anesthesia as they cut me and pulled my son from me; a final separation much like the one taking place today in this canoe.

His life threatened to be taken away before he took his first breath.

I gathered up what was left of his ashes and threw small handfuls in the lake along with flowers I had purchased at Vons market, which now seemed meaningless and unimportant amongst the beauty already there under the canopy. I watched as he floated along with the flowers, the ducks following and then as though it had all been rehearsed, his ashes drifted into a reed patch on the side of the lake. I knew without knowing the reeds were calling him to his final resting place and there he would be safe and protected.

Forevermore.

SHE

She is eighty years old and she has undaunted stretch marks
She still pulsates with life giving rhythms
Her hair has turned from auburn to gray
She is adaptable

She sees life with her heart
She hears God through her prayers
She already knows all there is to know
She is reliable

She is empowered by her womanhood
Her power frightens her so she gives it away
She is God's wonder of all creation
She is pliable

She talks about face lifts and tummy tucks
She thinks about the Universe and God
Life's currents have rendered her whole
She is viable

She is childhood and motherhood
She is earth's umbilical cord to heaven
She has survived her own holocaust
She is applaudable.

THUMBS

These thumbs are eighty years old this year

Deep crevices on the knuckles
Blood rushes through the protruding veins
Makes me pause to appreciate their sense of duty
They chose a life of struggle and strife over a life of leisure and spoils
They still stand pat, ready for duty in whatever form it comes
These thumbs have served for eighty years

Brave soldiers to the end.

MARCH 14, 2015

THURBER

My longest most successful relationship.
Eighteen years.

WORDS

Words hang in the gallery of my mind.
They are untouched and unused,
Gifts from other times and other places.
They are locked up, away from my grasp.
"*Precious Words*," the sign says.
"*Do Not Touch.*"

      Wordless poems have become my pastime lately.
      I see a child in his mother's arms today.
      He clings to her for his every need.
      His skin is the same as hers.
      I close my eyes to find the words.
      The words remain in their dust free cases.

I hear my son's voice.

"Love you, Mom," as he says goodbye.
No longer in my arms.
No longer clinging to me for his every need.
His skin is the same as mine.
No words.

      I visited the gallery again today,
      There is a new sign.
      "*Precious Words for Poets Only.*"
      I go back to my wordless poems
      And wait for the words.
      Maybe I will write a song.

My soul waits

Wrapped in a blanket of eternal light

Gently filled with God's grace.

Jean Johns lives in Santa Barbara, California

CPSIA information can be obtained
at www.ICGtesting.com
Printed in the USA
FSOW02n1427290416
19873FS